M000033495

# Horse & Dog

## *Adventures in Early California*

Short Stories & Poems by

Ransom A. Wilcox

Edited by Karl Beckstrand

Premio Publishing & Gozo Books
Midvale, UT, USA
PremioBooks.com

**Horse and Dog Adventures in Early California:**
Short Stories and Poems by Ransom A. Wilcox

*For Vanessa, Dylan, Jason, and Justin*

Premio Publishing & Gozo Books © 2013
Midvale, UT, USA
Library of Congress catalog number: 2013913405
ebook ISBN: 978-1301904747
ISBN: 978-0615856162

*The cover image is an actual photo of Ol' Blue. The author (or his brother "Teeter") is in the background.*

 PREMIO PUBLISHING

# Contents

# A Barn Full o' Proud

Y ou might say, for the times, I was a typical Sacramento Valley ranch boy. I could ride a horse bare-back at a flat-out run when I was eight years old. It wasn't long before I could herd our cows into the corral while standing on the horse. When I was fourteen, I was doing a man's work and earning a man's pay.

Feeling sorry for myself was not one of my weaknesses. But this morning, I was close to it. It was my birthday. By the time my dad and mom were up, I was already dressed. I looked directly at them as they said, "Good morning, David." I was disappointed but shrugged it off. They were hardworking ranch people trying to make a go of a small acreage. Even after my accident, they treated me the same. (Maybe they were a little more unfeeling than I thought they should be.) It seemed to me that my older sister got most of the attention. At least her clothes cost more.

But I knew where to find genuine love—in the most beautiful thing God ever made—sure as you're born. Let me tell you how I came to fall in love.

*Raking hay. Photo courtesy of Herb Grommeck*

Dad used to hire out each summer to come up with extra money for taxes. A couple of summers back, I joined him, working for a rancher we called "Big Bill" Baldwin.

It took plenty of hay to feed his cattle; it seems as though I spent months driving Dad's team with a mower round and round the alfalfa fields. The Pitman arm would chatter as it worked the blade back and forth across the stems. From the standpoint of looks, our old horses, Son and Tad, weren't much to brag about, but they were stayers. The railroad had put a stage line out of business. This team had been the leaders in a six-horse hitch. Now they looked a little drawn, and you could count their ribs.

After a few days of drying, hay was raked into windrows. Sometimes a baler followed down the rows and kicked out neatly baled hay. But some hay was stacked. A tall boom on a tripod was positioned next to a row. The loader on a hayrack would plunge a hayfork into the hay. My job was to drive the horse team that moved the fork's steel cable through a pulley, drawing the hay up to the boom arm. When the load reached the pulley, the loader would swing the arm over the stack and, when properly positioned, jerk the trip. The hay cascaded onto the top of the stack. A man on the stack spread the hay evenly (otherwise it would slide off). It was a source of pride to produce a tall, well-rounded stack.

One day, lightning struck the tripod and traveled from the boom through the cable, knocking me senseless. This was probably a good thing, because the horses tried to bolt. The whole contraption came down, which kept the horses from getting far, but I had to be untangled from the equipment.

I was mangled pretty badly. Mr. Baldwin paid the hospital bill, but my arm and hand were never the same after that. I didn't let it stop me. The next summer I was back on the job. By holding one rein in the crook of my arm, I could ease the strain that simple grasping put on my poor hand as the day wore on.

Mr. Baldwin owned the finest pair of Percheron draft horses I'd ever seen. They must have weighed about 1,400 pounds apiece. Charlie Scott, from up the valley, had been hired to drive this big team. He was a strapping fellow (he must have weighed over two hundred pounds), who was inclined to be somewhat of a braggart. Only about four years my senior, he let me know often that I was just a kid.

An old wagon chassis had been converted into a chuck wagon. On the noon break, it would be nearby to feed the crew. We had an hour for lunch because the teams required that much time to consume the hay and oats they needed.

Charlie claimed "his" team could out-pull and out-work any team on the spread. Waving his nose at Son and Tad, he said, "A good, stiff wind would blow them jackrabbits sideways."

Something like this went on nearly every time we nooned. I guess my dad got a little tired of the continual ribbing. One day he said, "Tell you what, Charlie. There's a hundred-acre field of hay mowed four days ago. I'll bet you a week's pay that my team of 'jackrabbits' will rake half of it before your team can."

"You gotta be kiddin'," said Charlie. "Those scrawny ewes would barely be starting by the time I finished. Tell you what—I'll give you two weeks' pay if your time is better than mine. Since yours is the slowest team, I'll lead off and let them eat my dust."

"How about passing?"

"That's a laugh—you can't pass what you can't catch! Pass anytime you get the chance."

"Inside?"

"Why not? You'll never get close enough."

The race was set for Saturday.

After work, I walked Son and Tad toward the corral to brush them down. Sam Cole, the colored cook, was watching Mr. Baldwin's prize stud cavorting around the field. It was a picture as the horse crow-hopped and kicked up his heels in sheer jubilation at being alive. As he ran around the pasture with his mane and tail fluttering in the wind, Sam said, "Man oh man, that black beauty is plumb full o' proud!" I agreed, but my eye was taken by something even more impressive in the corral—a thing of enchantment.

She was a sorrel filly with a mane and tail of pure palomino gold. Her large, lambent eyes were separated by a white blaze. Her dainty, white-stockinged legs seemed to let her float over the ground, almost angel-like. I figured if a cat could look at a king, it would be all right if I looked at a queen. To me, she was more than royalty—I was in love. But I had to take care of my team.

The next day, I showed up early for a proper introduction. Ginger was as sweet as she was pretty. After getting permission from Mr. Baldwin, I approached her, humming softly. Soon we were riding around the corral. She was so smooth—she was the only horse I trusted with the reins in my bad hand alone.

When Saturday came, my dad said, "Dave, you're

drivin' the team."

"Me? You've had more experience."

"You can handle it."

Dad could see my insecurity. "Have you ever had a reason to doubt my judgment?"

"No, sir."

"You know this team—and you've run the rake plenty—so I don't have to tell you how to do that. If you don't kick the trip at the right time, don't worry; you're not trying to win a prize for the straightest rows."

Charlie was positioned ahead of me. Dad whispered, "Hold old Son and Tad back a little. Don't give them their heads until I wave my hat." I wrapped one of the lines around my bad arm, and, at the signal, we were out.

In the first round, Charlie led by several lengths. When three-quarters of the field had been raked, Charlie was nearly an entire lap ahead of me. The turns were getting tighter as we moved closer to the middle of the field.

Both my arms ached from the strain of holding my team back, but my bum arm began to throb. I figured we had about six laps to go when I saw my dad swing his hat back and forth. I let up on the lines, and my team swung into a perfectly synchronized reaching gait that began eating up the distance between the Percherons and me. About three more laps would see the job done. Now my leg was giving me pain from the continual kicking of the trip lever.

By this time, I was right behind Charlie's team. Sweat darkened Son and Tad's coats. But Charlie's team was fighting for breath, sides heaving. Charlie gave one agonized look over his shoulder and began beating his team with the ends of his lines.

On the last lap, I cut inside Charlie's path. The crew was shouting. The wheels of the rake tore up clods and dust as they spun along. Coming down the last stretch, Charlie and I were almost neck and neck. Now I was oblivious to my arms and leg. I could see the post that marked the finish. It seemed to approach with maddening slowness.

I was afraid to take a good look at the team so close beside me. By this time, the draft horses had broken into a lumbering gallop as Charlie flayed their rumps with the lines. Even so, the team's position didn't seem to change.

I urged my team with a pleading voice and shook the lines over their straining backs. Their bellies got closer to the ground as those long legs moved with the smoothness of pistons, which belied the contraption behind them. Son and Tad knew they were in a race, and they seemed eager to get their noses under the wire first. Their necks reached out, and their manes flew back in the wind of their motion.

My team reached the finish nearly three lengths ahead of Charlie's. The whole crew was dancing up and down, whooping and yelling like Comanches. Old Son and Tad were still pulling at the bits as I stiffly got off the rig. About this time, Charlie's rig pulled up. He jumped from the seat and rushed at me. He gave me a shove that put me on my back and knocked the wind out of me. "You cheated on the turn! You cheated on the turn!" he yelled.

Mr. Baldwin and Dad grabbed Charlie by each arm. I got up slowly just as Mr. Baldwin said, "You're through here, Charlie. You damn near foundered a good team! Go to the cook shack, and get your time."

This wasn't a large community. Most everyone knew a little about everyone else. I knew that Charlie had been orphaned when he was twelve and that a crotchety uncle had assumed the unwanted job of raising him. I also knew that once you were fired by Mr. Baldwin, hardly any rancher in the valley would have you on his place. I saw crestfallen, embarrassed panic in Charlie's eyes. "Mr. Baldwin," I said, "don't fire Charlie. He might have won if I hadn't been fifty pounds lighter. It might not have been fair."

Charlie stood between the two men looking desperate and ashamed. It wasn't about a lost race or two weeks' wages anymore; he knew in his heart he'd been a poor loser and had used his size to push someone smaller.

Mr. Baldwin stared at me real hard, as though he were a little affronted at a kid butting into what should be a man's affair. After a moment, he said to Charlie, "Get over to that team, and take their harnesses off. I don't have to tell you how to cool them down. That pair cost me a thousand dollars. If I find they're ruined, I'll take it out of your future wages!"

Then Mr. Baldwin laid a big hand on my shoulder. With a sort of affection in his eye, he said, "David, I've seen you with that little quarter horse filly in the corral. You takin' a shine to that little mare?"

Well, I didn't know what to say.

"Since you've shown you've learned a little of what it takes to be a man today, I'd feel very proud if you'd accept Ginger as a gift from me."

Here I was, just a kid, and the most important man in the valley was paying me an honor. Not only that, he'd actually asked me to accept something that I'd never hoped to own in my wildest dreams. My throat was so tightened up that I couldn't get a word of appreciation out. I felt like a blockhead, just standing there.

Dad and Mr. Baldwin were looking at me with smiles on their faces. I looked over at the crew. They were all grinning and laughing. I knew they weren't laughing at me; they were just sharing the joy that infused my face. I turned tail and ran like a scared rabbit in the direction of the corral, where my new love waited with that proud neck arched. Her soft muzzle pushed toward me to be petted.

When Charlie finished his summer work for Mr. Baldwin, he came to work for us at Dad's invitation. He'd lost his cocky ways, and we hunted and fished together. Also, I think he was kinda stuck on Julia, my sister.

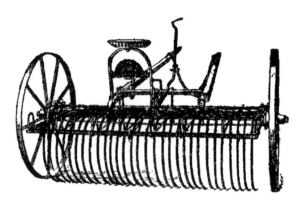

Today I was turning sixteen. I headed into the barn to see my Ginger. But where was she? My heart thundered. Could she have been stolen? My fear turned to shock when I found her standing in the sun by the ten-foot-wide doors. I stopped. She was decked out as I'd never seen her before.

As I approached, I could hardly believe the sight. There was a brand-spanking-new saddle on her back. I knew it was a Visalia hull—the best. And how she set it off! She had perfect conformation and seemed proud to be wearing it. A little sign said, "From Mom and Dad."

Hanging from the saddle horn was a fine pair of Justin boots. The note said, "Love, Julia." Those stinkers in the house hadn't said a word this morning; they had hardly given me the time of day. My cup of ecstasy was about as full as it could get—or so I thought.

But I had yet to experience the greatest thrill of all—a thrill that shook me down to my old, scruffy boots! Between the new Navajo saddle blanket and the saddle skirt was an envelope. I pulled it out and tore it open. Boy oh boy, that sneaking coyote Charlie Scott had stolen my Ginger out of the barn—behind my back! He and my folks had connived with Bill Baldwin, to breed my Ginger to that big, black stud. Ginger's foal would be fully pedigreed with a noble lineage going back six generations and registered in the studbook.

My semi-stunned condition must have been an entertaining scene. From the corner of my eye, I noticed Mom, Dad, Julia, and Charlie with smiles that nearly split their faces. "Happy Birthday!" they said.

As old Sam might have observed, that sunlit barn was surely "full o' proud!" Ginger turned her head and nudged my bum elbow with her velvety nose. She didn't care about pedigrees; she was just happy to see me!

# Ol' Blue

Death is so permanent, as someone once put it. It comes in many guises and locales. In my case, death was on the side of a rather steep hill. Death was a wild hog with tusks several inches long. In my haste to retreat from a charging wild animal, I had fallen flat on my face.

A pig that weighs over four hundred pounds is a frightening sight; the red hackles stand up straight, the eyes aflame with fury. Sharp tusks gleam like scimitars. There's a slaver of foam from the mouth and an intense grunt of irritation.

This was a wild sow with five or six little ones. She was in a killing mood and would protect her piglets with her life. In the process, she was willing—and aiming—to take mine. As I scrambled to get back onto my feet, I was sure my escape efforts would be futile.

Wild pigs have been a fact of life for centuries. The razorbacks of the South are notorious for their vicious attacks on dogs and men. Once a man is down, the razorbacks kill him and eat him on the spot.

In California, there are wild hogs from Ventura to all the way up beyond the state's northern border. These hogs are a hybrid of the European wild boar and domestic pigs gone wild in rough country. They raid farmers' crops, dig up golf courses, and tempt domestic pigs to join them in the wild.

I arrived at this lethal predicament while visiting my brother "Teeter" during the Great Depression of the 1930s. Teeter lived in the back country of Mendocino County in a cabin on the middle fork of the Eel River, ten miles from the nearest road.

Hunting wild hogs is a specialty in itself. Teeter did it as a matter of survival. Hogs are rarely seen. They have an acute sense of smell; they can detect a wild onion five inches below the ground.

Hog hunting involves a pack of specially trained dogs. Our pack consisted of four dogs. Buster, a black-and-white hound, was the tracker. His nose could pick up a week-old pig trace. Blue—a shaggy calico of gray, white, and bluish fur—was the acknowledged leader. Turk, a brown Lab, was the young one; he was long on courage and short on common sense. Molly, Turk's mother, was timid—except when a fight was in progress.

We rode mountain-bred horses that savvied steep terrain and thick brush. We lined out one frosty morning with Buster ranging ahead. At about ten o'clock, he let go with his telltale howl. He had come across hot pig scent. We dug in our heels and took off down the mountain and then went slipping and sliding across an opening.

The pack had closed in on something that hadn't run very far. "Sounds like a young one or a big sow with pigs," Teeter said. "If it's a sow, she won't retreat much."

Our technique was to let the dogs bay the pig. If the pig were small enough, we would give the dogs the order to catch. Then, instead of circling the quarry, the dogs would close in and attempt to hold the pig until we could get close.

Once there, we would leap off the horses, run in, and flip the pig on its side. Then we would gag the pig with a stick tied in the mouth (for our own protection). We'd tie a twenty-foot line to the hog's hind foot. Molly would lead, and the other three dogs would range behind to discourage a breakaway pig with a nip on the flanks.

Once we got the pig home, it would be put in a fenced yard and fed grain until it was mature enough to slaughter. If a hog was too big to lead out of the hills, it was shot, loaded on a horse, and then converted into ham, bacon, and sometimes sausage.

From the clamoring, we knew the dogs were facing a real fight. The terrain was steep and covered with dense buckbrush. We detoured around several patches of brush and finally came to the river. It was at about half-flood stage, so we had to go upstream to an area that was shallow enough to ford. The water was up to the saddle skirts. We rode with feet on the saddle horn to keep dry.

A path ran along the river. We followed this until we were below the commotion just up the hill. We ground reigned the horses. Teeter pulled his rifle from its boot and set off up the hill. The brush was dense but spotted with small openings here and there.

Teeter went to the left and followed a dim path that seemed to lead above the melee. I followed him a short distance to an outcrop with a view of the fight. The quarry was a huge, red sow. From the length of her tusks, I figured she was at least twelve years old. Her dugs were swollen, so I knew she had little ones. When we came into view, Turk charged the pig head-on. She caught him with her right tusk and sent him end over end at least eight feet in the air. We saw a spume of blood gush out where she had ripped his belly.

The sow broke and disappeared in the brush. I knew she wouldn't go far from her pigs. We split up. Teeter positioned himself above and was trying to get in a shot. I cut down the hill and, from the sounds above, figured I was below and beyond the pig. I entered a small opening on the right. This was steep terrain. The ground was reddish with clay and full of small, sharp rocks.

The sow sprang from the brush at about my level. I turned to run up to a small outcrop. In my panic, I drove too hard, and my feet slipped out from under me. I was the enemy, and I was momentarily helpless. I saw the sow set herself for the charge.

Teeter was working his way down from above. He saw her and let go a shot. Now a 30-30 has pretty good muzzle velocity, and an 85-grain bullet is a lot of lead. But I have seen a large buck take a hit and keep on going—which is just what this sow did. She was halfway to me. I imagined that white, glistening tusk going into my vitals. I seemed frozen at that point. Suddenly, out of nowhere, came a forty-pound, furry bundle of pure fury.

Ol' Blue, with mouth agape and his plume of a tail straight back, met that charging sow head-on. He was like an angel of mercy. Ten feet from the pig, he left the ground in a headlong dive. As pack leader, his job was to fasten onto a pig's nose while the other members of the pack grabbed an ear or other part.

The old saying "I couldn't believe my eyes" holds well here. Blue went for the nose and clamped down on it, and his momentum carried him beyond the pig and downhill. The sow lost her footing, flopped over on her side, and—with ol' Blue still fixed to her nose—slid down the hill. By the time Teeter shot a slug in at the sow's jawline, Buster had a hold of her ear, and Molly had locked onto the sow's hind leg. The sow expired with a series of convulsive jerks.

Teeter pushed Blue away from the sow's nose and proceeded to cut her throat. Blue walked over to me with a wide, happy grin. I took this panting bodyguard in my arms. My face went blank as I pictured what might have happened. Blue licked me back to the task at hand.

The sow was so heavy that we had to gut her on the spot. We brought in a horse, tied a rope to the sow, and dragged her to a short cliff on the hillside, from which we were finally able to get her on the saddle and lashed down.

Teeter, on the other horse, led out toward the river. Looking back, he saw Blue still up on the hill where the brawl had started. He called to him in a scolding voice. Blue dropped his head and tail momentarily, but he refused to budge from his position.

Teeter dismounted, and we both made our way back to the scene of engagement. Blue whined and looked at an area in the brush patch. When we got in closer, we saw Turk lying under the brush. He was still alive.

The tusk had ripped him from brisket to groin. One testicle dangled from its cord, but the tusk had not entered the abdominal cavity. We cut the cord, leaving on the hill that which could not be put back. Teeter took up Turk in his arms. "He'll probably bark in a high-bitched voice from here on out," he said as we started for home. I brought up the rear, behind the horse that carried the sow.

It was dark by the time we got home. Teeter's wife, Evelyn, boiled a needle and thread and sewed up the slash in Turk's belly. A little splash of sheep dip for disinfectant, and the operation was complete. Molly and Buster were waiting to be fed, but Blue was not to be found. We thought he might have been worn out and would come in later.

After supper, the dogs began to bark. As we stepped outside, we could see them heading for the lower gate to the pasture. We lit a lantern and followed.

At the gate, we saw a strange sight. We were looking at a miracle. Lined along the fence were five little pigs that had recently lost their mother. Ol' Blue stood proudly in the background. Being an Australian shepherd, it never occurred to him that it wasn't his job to bring this wild little flock home.

The trail was rough, tortuous, and sometimes very steep. Yet, somehow, he had herded these pigs through the darkness. He was so weary that he could hardly stand. We opened the gate, and he guided his little charges through it.

Teeter surmised that Blue had stayed with the pigs until they had gotten used to him. With their mother gone, they may have been willing to stay close to him.

About a week later, Turk was up and around and as spry as usual. We decided to scout the other side of the river. Beyond the ford, we followed a trail upstream. As we forded a small tributary, we saw two salmon spawning in a riffle above the crossing. We didn't have a gig to spear them with, but we sure wanted a change of diet from pork or venison. Teeter suggested he take the rifle and move up to a hole above the riffle where the fish were spawning. As he got set, I was to throw a rock in the vicinity of the fish. When they got near the hole, he would blast at them with the rifle, hoping the concussion would stun them.

When I thought he was set, I picked up a rock about the size of a baseball and winged it at the fish. It was a lucky throw, because I hit a fish right in the head. The fish flipped straight up in the air. It was stunned, and when it landed in the water, it was crosswise of the stream. One powerful whip of its tail sent it toward the shore. It crossed a small sandbar and ended up flopping around in the shallow backwater.

"Go get 'im, Blue!" I shouted. Blue dove off the bank and dragged the fish onto land. I heard the gun go off above. The next thing I knew, a belly-up fish came floating down the stream. Blue was off the bank again. He grabbed the fish and dragged it to the bank.

Those were good times in beautiful country. Redwoods and towering firs covered the hills. In the summer, Evelyn would wheel the baby carriage out into the sun in front of the house. My niece, Elaine, was Blue's great love. He would lie down alongside the buggy with his muzzle on his paws.

There were cougars, wildcats, and range bulls in the area. The worst menace to small children was town dogs that collected in packs. These dogs attacked children, sheep, calves, turkeys, and other dogs. But as long as Blue was on watch, the baby was safe.

*Photo courtesy Andreas Krappweis*

I drove back to my home in the Bay Area. The next year, I returned to the mountains to visit my brother. It was near Christmastime. There was a foot or two of snow over the Low Gap Pass on the road west to Fort Bragg.

When I pulled up to the front of the house, I sensed that something was wrong. No dog announced my approach with barking. I knocked on the door. My brother opened it but did not greet me with a hug or a handshake. There was a woebegone look on his face. "Blue is dying," he said.

I followed him into the house. Blue lay on an old quilt behind the wood-burning stove. "How yuh doin', old-timer?" I said. Blue knew me and responded with a weak thump of his tail. His ribs stood out through his patchwork coat. I noticed that one of his hind feet looked as though all the tendons had been cut and the blood supply severed. "What happened?" I asked, averting my nose from the stench.

"You know the woven wire fence running down toward the barn?" said Teeter. "He went to jump it, but while his nose and front paws were going over top strands of the fence, his back foot was going into the square of wire below. As his weight dropped on the other side of the fence, the foot brought the second strand up and got trapped between two wires. I found him the next morning hanging by his foot. There was snow on his back, and he seemed almost lifeless. In his torment, he almost chewed a post in two. That was two days ago. It's only a matter of time until the blood poisoning takes him."

"Are you just going t' stand around and watch him die in agony?" I asked.

"I haven't got the guts to shoot him."

"It's inhumane," I said. "Bring me the rifle. Let's get it over with."

When we called, ol' Blue struggled to his feet and followed us out the back door. His head sagged, and that great plume of a tail was at half-mast. As we approached the barn, Evelyn came running from the house. "You're not going to kill that dog!" she thundered. "Might as well shoot me or Elaine!"

Teeter knew I had ambition to be a doctor. After a couple of years of medical training, lack of funds had put a stop to that dream. "Doc," he said, "do you think you could amputate that foot?"

"What—me?" I said. "There's no anesthetics, no surgical tools—and I've never operated on anything before." Once in college, we spread-eagled an alley cat. After giving it chloroform, we cut it open and watched the heart beat. That was the extent of my experience.

"Haven't you read about surgical procedures?"

"Yeah, but that was just theory—a far cry from an actual operation!"

"You still know more about it than I do."

I looked at my friend, Blue. "If I operate, the procedure could kill him."

Finally, I said, "He's going to die anyway. What have we got to lose?" Looking at Evelyn, I said, "If Evelyn agrees, she won't blame us so much for his death."

"If you take the foot off, at least he's got a chance," she said.

"I think he's got a good chance," said Teeter. "He's got more fight—more guts—than I have. My money's on Blue."

It was decided. Evelyn was off to get her uncle and an old hillbilly she and Teeter called Shag to help. But what did I have to work with? There was a hunting knife, honed to a razor's edge. Evelyn had some needles and thread. The rest of my tools consisted of a hacksaw, a pair of pliers, a rasp, and scissors. As before, the disinfectant was sheep dip.

At first, Evelyn's uncle protested. "You're crazy. Count me out—I want no part of it!"

"Who you tryin' to kid?" said Evelyn. "You're just chicken—like I am—afraid of a little blood."

Down by the barn was a ten-by-ten platform that was supposed to be a tent floor. We wrapped Blue in a canvas with just his nose and his bad leg sticking out and then laid him on the platform. Evelyn had tied the other dogs up by the house, but at the last minute, she let Turk loose to watch over his friend.

Evelyn's uncle and Shag had the dog firmly pinned to the platform. Teeter handed me the knife. My stomach felt queasy as I looked at the leg. Here I was, about to cut into the quivering flesh of a friend—a friend who had put his life between death and me. He was only a dog, just an animal, I reminded myself.

No. Here lay the epitome of courage, compassion, loyalty, and unswerving devotion. My hand shook a little.

"Let's be done with it," said Teeter.

I realized that emotion had no place in this situation. This was the time for intense concentration. I slashed into the muscle of the upper thigh. Blood spurted as I cut across the femoral artery. I half expected Blue to cry out in pain. He never let out so much as a whimper. He didn't even try to pull the leg out from under my hands.

"Pinch that artery with the pliers," I said to Teeter. "Good. Give me the needle." I tied a clumsy knot that seemed to shut off most of the blood.

I'd made my cut at an angle toward the bone. I did the same on the other side, ending up with tapered flaps of skin. Now the white of the femur was exposed. I held the lower end of the bone with my left hand. With the hacksaw, I cut the bone off high up in the v of the flaps. The saw left a sharp, erose bone end. With the rasp I rounded the bone off as best I could. All this time, there wasn't a whimper from Blue.

It came to me that I may have lost the patient from shock. I shoved my hand up under the canvas and laid it against Blue's upper ribs. Nothing in the world felt as good as the thump of that great heart against my hand.

The sweat bathed my face and dripped off the end of my nose. With needle and thread, I sewed the two flaps together. This involved using the pliers to force the needle through the tough skin. After the sew job, I wrapped the leg in strips from a sheet Evelyn had furnished. I made a boot from some heavy material and tied it to a sling over the dog's back.

"That's it," I said. "Unwrap him."

Evelyn had been watching from the kitchen window. When she saw the operation was over, she approached with a little fear, half expecting to see a dead dog.

Blue lay exposed on the canvas. His red tongue licked his lips. He looked up at me. His tail banged against the floor. Then he heaved himself to his feet, supporting himself on his three legs. Turk barked, and the rest of us cheered like a bunch of ninnies. This wasn't a humorous occasion, but Blue got a smile out of each of us.

Little Elaine had learned to walk. As she came out, Blue hobbled over to her and pressed his shaggy body against her. Evelyn kneeled beside them and folded Blue in her arms. He licked her salty tears, his tail whipping back and forth. Then he let out a joyful yip.

He had to relieve himself, so he hobbled up to a bush and lifted his leg. Unfortunately, he didn't know that his left leg was gone. He fell down with a slight yelp.

Well, he was famous, and I was famous, throughout the county. He lived to go on many a hunt—on three legs. Blue had lost a leg but not his courage. Nor had he lost any of the many who loved him.

# For Blue

*I was down, beaten, and depressed—*
*So many troubles on my mind.*
*No friends came by to offer a hand—*
*Not that they meant to be unkind.*
*My dog came slowly to where I sat,*
*Head in hands, bowed down with care.*
*He looked at me, misery in his gaze;*
*My sorrows and hurt he too would share.*
*First he licked my hands and face*
*And pressed his shaggy body to me.*
*Then he nuzzled his head on my chest,*
*And left it there to warm just me.*
*He may look rumpled, uncombed at times.*
*He may not have a pedigree.*
*But he never quits, never leaves a job—*
*And one of those is loving me.*

# Quiet Waters

*Let me come with you, inside your head.*
*I will stay far back*
*In a quiet corner.*
*And I will be still until you call to me.*
*I am a living picture*
*Of serenity and beauty,*
*Treasured in your memory.*
*I shall wait to be*
*Called forth*
*When your soul needs calming.*

*I came into your mind*
*Through your eyes:*
*Eyes that were busy—*
*Busy looking*
*And seeing*
*More than the eye*
*Was seeing—*
*Seeing a fragile*
*Depth of awe*
*And being swept into a whirl*
*Of remembering pleasant scenes.*

*Because you chose to walk*
*The path beside me,*
*I became part of you*
*In a way deep and secure.*
*For I am a brook.*
*I talk to you*
*As we ramble along*
*Together.*
*My voice*
*Is the tinkle*
*Of clear freshness*
*Flowing over the stones,*
*Beneath the ripples,*
*Below the pool.*

*And you will pause,*
*Enthralled,*
*At the willow-shrouded*
*Stillness*
*That lies above*
*My quiet waters.*

# My Little Girl

*I saw a blithe, bright spirit*
*Behind a pair of roguish eyes.*
*Oh lovely, lovely spirit,*
*You've made my life a paradise.*

*Where did you come from, Angel—*
*A land of sweetness and light?*
*Since you stole into my heart,*
*My life's been oh, so bright.*

# Character

*Character is the shining armor that protects you from*
*yourself. Without it, you are the victim of temptations*
*that destroy your health and your reputation.*
*Do your duty and your job, and you will lend a strength*
*and dimension to your character that no man or event*
*can destroy.*

# Friendship

*What art thou to me, my bosom friend?*
*A strength to my soul in times of stress.*
*Often hast thou taught me not to bend*
*To deeds that bring remorse, regret.*

*A breath, respite, and rest descend*
*In friendship's harbor—all is calm.*
*No time or season ever ends*
*The soothing of thy balm.*

*Thy wealth cannot be bought or sold;*
*Nor can mere mortals own*
*The warmth, the ecstasies, that spring*
*From friendship's caring tone.*

*Thy constancy every wall crosses.*
*Despair quits all our senses.*
*Pure joy replaces all our losses,*
*And love tears down all fences.*

*Loneliness is no longer sowed.*
*Shared experiences expand*
*As we walk an endless road.*
*New horizons fill the land.*

# To the Redwoods!

*Ye beings of infinite grace and calm,*
*Ye trees,*
*Swaying, soothing symphonies*
*From each vagrant breeze,*

*Roots embedded*
*In God's created soil,*
*Straining through droughts and seasons*
*With endless toil,*

*Warmth and color*
*Against a once-barren sky,*
*Solace and comfort*
*To a world-weary eye,*

*Golden sunlight*
*Filtered through branches wide*
*Casts a spell of beauty*
*O'er the countryside.*

*Flitting, shiny spirits*
*Swoop o'er needle-littered ground*
*And scold the saucy chipmunks*
*That everywhere abound.*

*Oh trees, whose faith has reared*
*A monument to God,*
*Whose elements for beauty*
*Come from rock and sod,*

*To have thy faith, unswerving,*
*In a storm-tossed grove,*
*It is peace and sureness*
*Of God's unfailing love.*

# Mother

*The troubles in your heart*
*No one can know,*
*Or how bravely you've smiled*
*On a world of woe.*
*How often in the weary,*
*Long vigils of the night*
*You've grieved and hoped and prayed*
*That your love will make things right.*
*But no matter what fate may bring,*
*Of one thing I can be sure:*
*That you will never, ever forsake me*
*For you are my mother forevermore.*

# To a Granddaughter

*Lines have been written*
*To the glories of the glistening night,*
*To the splendor of the rising sun's*
*Quick delight.*

*The moon and stars have moved the bards*
*To lines of rhyme and prose,*
*As also has the beauty of*
*A delicate, budding rose.*

*But you, more beautiful than these,*
*Make mute my feeble pen.*
*No mere words can e'er suffice*
*To paint beauty's garden.*

*You are like a garden of flowers,*
*Gentle as the breeze*
*That softly stirs the petals*
*And moves the fragile leaves.*

*You invade the senses like odors sweet*
*From nightshade and pale moonflower,*
*Opening with innocent stealth*
*Around a latticed bower.*

*I dare not move*
*For fear the spell will go,*
*And you, so beautiful,*
*Will vanish in its glow.*

*For it's not your hair or eyes*
*That move me so,*
*Nor the beauty of your smile,*
*Where dimples come and go,*

*But you—just you.*
*How can I tell you how I feel*
*About your gentle ways, your glow*
*And sweet appeal?*

*The very heart of who you are—*
*Your warmth, your willingness to share—*
*Makes all who know you love you and*
*All who know you care.*

*My halting lips cannot express*
*How your presence brings a thrill.*
*Words fail.*
*My heart stands still.*

# Immortality

Your life might be humdrum, the same old sixes and sevens day after day. Worldly thrills no longer bring you happiness. You may suffer from spectatoritis, which demeans your personality (you become a bore). Spectatoritis is the result of a natural focus on self and a cessation of study or output. The chronic spectator is a watcher, not a doer.

A happy life is counter intuitive—easy *doesn't* do it. Quality living and longevity are not solely a matter of nutrition, activity, diversion, and rest. The capacity for logical thinking must also be nourished. The mind affects the body, and the body affects the mind. If your life is not challenging and fulfilling, then you are being shortchanged. To truly live, the human soul must create.

I envy master creators—the artists, the musicians, the singers, the sculptors, the poets—gifted people who have left enduring stepping-stones on the path of human development. We who live and function on a lower echelon must remember that most artists, scientists, and other masters were once average minds—but they practiced. To emulate great minds is to progress to a superior plane.

Creating requires work. Build a table. Write music, or master a musical instrument. Paint. Write a piece of lyric poetry. Dance—interpret various rhythms with your body and spirit. Research your family roots. Learn to swim. Learn the names of plants or birds. Do something that impacts other people positively. Be a trusted source of information in a chosen field. Build a friendship by serving. Be your most beautiful self. Be an expert listener.

Life is filled with wonders and mysteries to be explored. The greatest existence comes not from food or possessions or people or power—but from being a creator— humbly adding your unique experiences to the world.

Everyday people can cast off shallow, selfish pursuits that destroy the capacity to imagine, to solve, and to excel. It is possible with regular, daily steps. As your intelligence expands, your universe expands. Stretching toward a noble goal brings a certain euphoria—a joy and a fulfillment with a godlike quality—a glimpse at unending horizons. Thrilled, you will inspire others to seek new activities, perspectives, and strengths.

This, then, is the key to immortality: to grow in stature, to understand and help others, and to be an instrument that expands vision and love. In creating, you will know a fulfillment that can be known only by those who live this way.

An atom of specialized matter called life exists in one form or another forever. You may have only one life—but who says it can't have lasting impact? Create something and become immortal!

# Happiness

Happiness is a quality that eludes typical quantitative analysis. You can enjoy prolonged happiness only by giving it away. The more happiness you give away, the more you have. Strange, isn't it?

When you think you are being made happy by acquiring material possessions, you may soon find that this process is like taking a drug. The more you have, the more you want. It always takes a little more to make you think you will be happier. This is a subtle form of deception. When you base your happiness on your possessions, if what you own is swept away, your happiness disappears with it.

So learn this well: do not pursue happiness as an end in itself. Happiness will come to you abundantly when you dedicate your life to making others happy. You must serve and help others face the trials and disappointments that come to all of us. This is the mystical key that opens the door to an ecstatic experience.

# ABOUT THE AUTHOR

**Ransom Adrian Wilcox** was born in Taber, Alberta, Canada, in 1907 to David Adrian and Agnes Southworth Wilcox. He was the sixth of seven children. Because Rance was sickly, the family moved to the warmer climate of California. The family was part of a group of Latter-day Saints (Mormons) that bought land in Vina, north of Chico.

For the most part, Wilcox's stories are autobiographical (though it was his younger brother who was crippled—by polio—and there was no gift of a mare).

Financial hardship forced the Wilcox family to move often in search of work. The family lived in Vacaville, Pope Valley, Gridley, Ukiah, Redwood Valley, Sebastopol, and Oakland. They farmed and tended sheep, cattle, horses, pigs, turkeys, and hens. They cured ham in a smokehouse and did a lot of hunting and fishing. Once, to escape a charging boar, Wilcox stuck a pole he was carrying into the ground and climbed up! One season the family lived in a tent while the men worked cutting hay. Every year at harvest time, all

*Wilcox's parents: David & Agnes*

the family members picked apples. Wilcox joined his father and brothers for a year in Arizona, building a school on an American Indian reservation.

In 1935, Wilcox married and began studying to be a chiropractor. But the Great Depression put his studies on hold. He tried several enterprises to support his family. Most failed. So did his marriage.

In 1943, Wilcox enlisted in the army. Because of his hunting background, his superiors had him train soldiers in gunnery and target practice. Just before his unit was to go fight overseas, Wilcox got the flu. He missed the boat—literally—and was honorably discharged.

Between more failed marriages, Wilcox completed his studies and opened a chiropractic practice just off Union Square in San Francisco. He took his kids to see Coit Tower, Fisherman's Wharf, Seal Rock, Smuggler's Cove, the Presidio, Fleishhacker Zoo, and football games at Kezar Stadium. Later he moved to Hayward and opened a practice on B Street.

Wilcox's friends called him Ray (for R. A.) or Doc. Besides writing, Wilcox was an excellent dancer. He enjoyed singing and was good with his hands. He loved to walk in the great outdoors.

Near the end of his life, Wilcox joked about leaving his body to science. "I'm sure they can use my brain. It's in perfect condition—never been used." In a letter to his daughter, he wrote, "In my heart I have no hatred or dislike for anyone. In my career I have eased many a person's pain and suffering."

Wilcox died of cancer in 1992 and is buried in Ukiah, California. His novel, *To Provoke the Eyes of His Glory*, will be out in 2014.

# More adventures from
## PremioBooks.com
Many in Spanish & English with pronunciation guide

Crumbs on the Stairs

Bad Bananas (cookbook)

Why Juan Can't Sleep

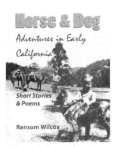

Horse & Dog Adventures

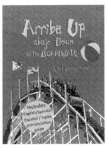

Arriba Up, Abajo Down

She Doesn't Want the Worms

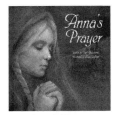

Anna's Prayer
Non-fiction

FREE ebook: It Ain't Flat

Sounds in the House: A
Mystery

Nationally-lauded language and activity books and ebook mysteries
(Horn Book blog, *ForeWord Reviews, School Library Journal*) with
Hispanic, white, black & Asian characters (for 3 years & up); also via
Amazon, B&T, B&N, Brodart, Follet/BWI, Ingram.

### FREE online books: MulticulturalKidsBooks.com

Title/
ISBN: _____ (circle): Engl, Span, biling! Quantity _____ at **\$7.95**/book = _____

Some titles are only available in English. See Premiobooks.com

Title/
ISBN: _____ Engl, Span, biling! Quantity _____ at \$ _____ /book = _____

Title/
ISBN: _____ Engl, Span, biling! Quantity _____ at \$ _____ /book = _____

Title/
ISBN: _____ Engl, Span, biling! Quantity _____ at \$ _____ /book = _____

Title/
ISBN: _____ Engl, Span, biling! Quantity _____ at \$ _____ /book = _____

Title/
ISBN: _____ Engl, Span, biling! Quantity _____ at \$ _____ /book = _____

Title/
ISBN: _____ Engl, Span, biling! Quantity _____ at \$ _____ /book = _____

USPS Media shipping: \$1.98 (for 1 book. Add \$.50 for each additional). For volume/expedited/credit card orders, see **Premiobooks.com**

All books **\$7.95.** Order with check or money order (mail. 15% restocking fee for returns): **Total:** _____

Name: _____

Premio Publishing & Gozo Books
648 W. Wasatch Street
Midvale, UT, 84047, USA
801-953-3793
info@premiobooks.com

Address: _____

_____

City _____ State: _____ Zip: _____

Made in the USA
Charleston, SC
03 July 2014